# Texting for Love

## A Guide for Attracting the Perfect Guy Through Texting

By Danielle A. Fox

# Table of Contents

# Introduction

Can texting really be the key to your romantic future? Can you really find love through the simple method of communication that we have all come to use daily? You might be surprised to learn that a few well placed and well thought out texts can be the key to a bright and beautiful future with somebody. Texting truly can be the key to love in your future, so get on board!

Though texting used to be something with a negative connotation, it has quickly become an effective and accessible way of communicating. It's simple, it's quick, and it's a great way to convey your message without much effort at all. Can this simple but effective method of communication really apply to dating and attracting the guy of your dreams? Absolutely!

### Texting Can Open the Gates Easily

When you are first getting to know somebody, that first face-to-face meeting can be tough! You might feel as though you are stuck in an uncomfortable situation or you might feel quite a bit of anxiety. You might simply be unsure of what to say or how to act... This is where texting can really come in handy! It helps take away that anxiety and apprehension and instead allows you to focus on what you want to say.

This can make for a great way of capturing attention or being the person that you really want to be. You can act a bit more outgoing and let go of your inhibitions when you are using texting to communicate. This makes for a good foundation and platform for which dating can follow naturally. In essence, texting can offer you that great start that you might not have otherwise enjoyed!

So you might think of texting as an impersonal form of communication, but this is not true! This might be the best way to build attraction and anticipation, and can really help to create a budding romance. Though you may not feel comfortable with that first date, texting can help to open the doors and set a good tone beforehand. Try this with your next potential relationship and watch it work for you!

*So let's get started learning why texting can work FOR you and let the attraction build for a successful dating future!*

# Chapter 1 - Basic Texting Rules

You might wonder what's okay to say and what's not. You might feel as though all of a sudden texting takes on a whole new meaning. You might freeze when you look at your phone and think that this next text message could determine your romantic fate. Stop! There's no reason to panic and you have everything to gain! But you do need to keep a few things in mind.

If you want to enjoy the excellent communication of texting where dating is concerned then you need to keep a few basic rules in mind. These aren't intended to hold you back, but rather make your experience a more enjoyable and successful one. If you can keep these at the forefront and really focus on sending out well thought out texts, then this can be the catalyst to great things ahead.

### Embrace Texting in the Right Way

Here are a few rules that ensure your texting conversations and communication overall is successful and works FOR you:

- **Always read your text aloud before you send it:** Though you won't always have to do this as you progress, it's a good idea at first. You want to be sure that it not only makes sense and flows, but also that it doesn't put too much out there. Texts are meant to be shorter and more concise, and so you want to leave a bit to the imagination. That being said you want to read it and be sure that it evokes interest and that it will get the person on the receiving end to want to chat more. Always read it out loud to be sure of the message, especially at first!

- **Try not to be too emotional when you text:** The more emotional that you are the more information that you put out there. The more that you share through a text, the more work that it feels like for the reader. When it comes to texting within a dating situation, you want to keep it interesting and make them want to learn more. So put your emotions aside no matter what you may be feeling, or wait until later when you have calmed down. Stressful texts never work!

- **Never text when intoxicated:** Though we all know that this is a bad idea in theory, we tend to test the limits of this in practice. Texting when you are drunk in any capacity will never lead to good things. You may say things you can't take back or you may even do things that you regret later on. Put the phone aside or have a friend take it from you if you are drinking and save your texts for the next day when you are sober.

- **Be yourself and let go of your inhibitions:** Though you do want to put thought into the texts, particularly at first, you also want to let go a bit. Have fun with this form of communication and embrace what it can do for your love life. Let go of your inhibitions and be the person that you really want to be but may be too shy to embrace. This is your shot at getting things started on the right foot so go for it!

- **Smile while you text and that will show through:** Along with a well thought out text a happy and positive text can be a great thing. Try to feel good about what you are saying and smiling when you write it and send it can help. Not only does this get you into the right frame of mind, but it can also serve well in terms of the receiver being interested in what you have to say. It really does work!

# Chapter 2 - Why Is Texting So Effective?

You may wonder what it is about texting that makes it so effective in this capacity. Most girls were able to get dates just fine before texting, so why is it that this so very important now? It's a valid question and yet when you see firsthand just how well it can work, you will be convinced! Though we all have different personalities and agendas, texting can work FOR us when other forms of communication can tend to do just the opposite.

Texting gives us that forum to be able to build anticipation, and this goes a long way to help us get that hot guy! You may have never met this guy or you may be very newly dating but when you send a few well-placed texts, it can really build up the anticipation for that next meeting. You start to think about the guy more and you start to feel excited when you have a text come in.

### Anticipation and Clear Communication Set an Excellent Staring Point

Along the same lines, you also experience that joy of getting a text and starting to really think about him. You are anticipating what the date will be like or what he might text you next. You are getting to know him in a whole new way and it's really fun and carefree. Though fewer words are exchanged than over the phone or email, that's the whole point of it---you are saying what you really WANT to say in a much more to the point way!

So the reason that texting works is that it helps to naturally build up that attraction through flirting and very clear communication. You may even end up dating him because he was so interesting to you over texts that you wouldn't normally date this type of guy! This is an exciting new form of flirting and really sets an excellent foundation for the two of you.

If used properly texting can kick things off on the right foot and really keep them going. You may find that you think about each other more and that you have a mode by which to communicate no matter what you are doing throughout the day. You can get him to think about you too and that goes back and forth. So this sets a great stage for great things to come and a very open communication in the relationship too!

**How Can Texting Work Against You?**

Though you have nothing to be afraid of and have everything to gain, you do need to be mindful that there are some ways that texting can actually work against you.

It's not anything that should hold you back, but you do need to be mindful of these things. Consider these your sort of warnings or guidelines that help you to ensure that you make the right choices when you want to text a guy.

As you know, texts tend to be a short and sometimes a very misguided form of communication. Though you may not realize it, the message that you are trying to send can often be interpreted in a completely different way than you intended it. Knowing that you must be mindful of the way you say things and what the he could take it as.

### Be Aware and Not Letting Things Hold You Back

If you want to be sure that you send the text message that you intend to, then think through these things. Again don't over think this, but just be aware for the best possible texts to encourage the process and never hurt it.

- **It is often open to a lot of misinterpretation:** This is by far the most common issue with texting in general. Since there are often so few words to convey your message, that usually means that there is a lot that can be read into it. Not only that, but texting doesn't necessarily allow him to really understand your tone. So the very benefits of texting (being an easy and effective form of communication because it's so brief) can also hold you back, so just be aware of this particularly when you are first sending text messages to guys you are attracted to.

- **You may not be sending the message that you think you are:** This has a lot to do with not being able to see the tone and emotions of the reader, and vice versa. When you send a message you may mean one thing but he might interpret it as something totally different. So try to keep it to the point and just think through any misread message that may come up. Most of the time, when you are sending the flirty and fun types of messages this isn't a problem, but better to think it through especially at first!

- **Sometimes it turns you into somebody that you really don't want to be:** This is particularly true if you get carried away or if you break the rule and send a text when you are drinking. Never get too overly aggressive when texting a guy you're attracted to. Be yourself, have fun with it, but keep the text messages carefree and fun for a much better message sent AND received. The key to successful texts within this stage is to smile when sending them, keep them light and carefree, and then you never risk the possibility of any of these things happening.

- **If you aren't yourself then you are misrepresenting yourself and that can backfire:** Sure you want to cast aside your inhibitions and throw yourself into this head-on, but try not to misrepresent yourself. It's all about having fun, but don't try to be somebody that you are not! This will always backfire on you in the end! Sure try to think outside the box, be creative, and enjoy texting through the dating and attraction phase by all means—but if you put lies or misrepresentations out there then he may end up very disappointed or deceived.

# Chapter 3 - What Are You Doing Wrong? Top Mistakes

Have you ever opened yourself up to texting and fell short? Did you ever think that you had a really good dialogue and vibe going only to find that texting put a wrench in it? So many people feel a bit fearful about texting when it comes to dating and relationships because they're worried about past patterns showing themselves again. Forget about what you thought you did wrong, and focus on the biggest mistakes out there.

These are the top mistakes across the board, and to be honest we've all been guilty of them. Though they seem innocent enough, when you really think about it you can see how they made things go wrong. So if you ever sent a text in the past only to never hear from the guy again, it's time to pay attention to what went wrong.

When trying to land your guy, these are the mistakes that you want to avoid. If you made them in the past then you understand why your intentions fell flat. Here's why they are always going to work against you.

### Trying to be Too Familiar Too Early

Sure you want to be yourself and yes you want to leave your inhibitions at the door. Yes there is a lot to be said for being proactive or somewhat aggressive, but there is such a thing as TOO aggressive. If you don't want to scare off the guy that you are texting with then by all means be sure that you aren't too overly familiar. This is an instant turn off!

This may signal a lot of different things to him, none of which are positive. They may think that you are easy or desperate. He might even think that you are too clingy. So be outgoing and have fun? Yes absolutely! However if you come on too strong too early in the process this will almost always end up in total disaster. Save a little bit for later and be slightly mysterious at the beginning to keep the interest going.

### Sending the Overly Evasive Text

Sending an overly evasive text is just as bad as being too aggressive in the beginning when you first meet. This tells him absolutely nothing, and this can be quite frustrating and turn guys away! Sure you want to be a bit mysterious and try to have fun with getting to know each other, but if you are too evasive this can be construed as being standoffish or even snotty. That's definitely not what you want to end up with!

Being overly evasive means that you give absolutely no information about yourself or what you want. It's almost as if you are giving him a reason to not to even text you back in the first place and that's not a good place to start from. Be slightly mysterious, have fun, don't put ALL your cards on the table, but don't try to be too mysterious either. Finding a fine balance comes with experience, but try to not to be so evasive that he thinks you're not interested.

### Next Steps with Your Texts

Another thing to watch for is being monotone or having absolutely no emotion or fun with your texts. If a guy feels that you are just going through the motions then he will tag you as boring from the start. And often times, it's very hard to change a guy's impression of you. You want to keep it light and fun, and also try to make your texts lead towards next steps. A date, a chance meeting, or just some fun conversation is among the things that you should be thinking through with the texts that you send.

When you can get to that place to evoke interest or to push along to one of your desired outcomes, then that's when your texts are successful. This is not just an informative or one word answer text when it comes to dating and relationships. So be sure that you are in this to have fun and to show him what you are all about, and what you want. Direct texts that show some sort of emotion and push for some sort of next step are the most successful ones!

# Chapter 4 - How to Put Myself Out There If I'm Shy?

If you are more of an introvert or just a shy person then you may think that texting is for other people. Simply not true! If you want to have a little fun with this then you can too, but it's up to you to invest this time into yourself. You need to bring yourself out of your shell so to speak, and texting can truly be the best way to do that—but be ready to take things up a notch!

Even if you're shy, you can still use texting as a fun and effective way of finding the perfect guy too! This may be a bit more difficult at first as it's about getting outside of your comfort zone. Once you can do that, then you are opening yourself up to all sorts of possibilities. The thing to remember though is that nobody else can do this for you, and that you must be ready to try a new adventure!

### *This May Be Hard at First But It Will Pay Off!*

Sure you might feel a bit uncomfortable at first. Sure this may be a bit tough to master or to find that courage and confidence within yourself. Sure it's going to perhaps result in a few mistakes along the way. This can however be a learning experience about your limits as much as it is about relationships in general. Just be willing to learn and to see where texting can take you.

Sometimes you follow the lead of the guy that you're texting with, and sometimes you want to take the lead. As you build up more texting experience within this capacity you will also gain more confidence. So keep a few things in mind to help you to enjoy texting that can lead to getting a hot guy on a date, even if you are the biggest wallflower in the world!

Here is how you make texting work well for you even if you are shy:

- **Be willing to work outside of your comfort zone:** This is going to take you outside of your comfort zone, perhaps like nothing else before. You are going to enjoy this experience but you have to allow yourself to do so. Be willing to do something that makes you stretch a bit as a person and be open to the experience that comes along with it. Go in with an open mind and a good attitude and you CAN make it work. Know that it may not feel comfortable at first, but building experience will help it to feel more like something that you do naturally and successfully.

- **Be open to trying new ways of talking that you have never done before:** When you talk to a guy that you are attracted to face-to-face you will probably fall back into your shy self. When you talk to a guy that you are attracted to over text however, then you may find that this is by far the best way to be your fun loving self. Embrace this type of technology for letting you put down your walls and really take the time to chat it up with the right person guy. This can help you to come out of your shell and really help to take the anxiety out of that first date or meeting. This form of communication can be the key to a whole new you and help you to finally find the perfect guy that you want to date!

- **Take on the persona of somebody that you want to be and run with it:** So many of us, particularly those that are shy, want to try to be somebody that we are not. We hear numerous times how people take on a certain persona to get them through a stressful situation, so why not do it here? If you have always wanted to be a certain way or to be a certain type of person but you felt afraid to try, then this is your opportunity. You can really be more extroverted, fun loving, and adventurous if you embrace texting while engaging with a guy. So be ready to be somebody that you have never had the courage to be, for there is so much possibility that lies ahead for you!

# Chapter 5 - The Right Way to Grab His Attention

So the moment of truth has come up on you and now it's up to you to find those words that will grab his attention. You know that you want to go on a date with him and you are definitely attracted to him, but you don't know what to say to convey that early on. These types of scenarios present themselves all the time and it may evoke a bit of anxiety into the process.

If you have never used texting to try and get a date, or if you have never done so successfully then this is your time to shine. The key is to come up with a great opener that will grab his attention and keep making him want to learn more. The idea is that you want to introduce yourself, but more importantly want to make him want to spend some time with you. In almost every situation, the opener can sometimes be the hardest part.

### Finding the Right Words Is So Important

So if you find yourself at a crossroads where you simply aren't sure of how to find the right words to grab his attention, there are a couple of things to keep in mind. Always be natural but do be sure that you are saying something interesting that captivates him and makes him want to learn more about you. Here are some helpful tips to finding that perfect opener:

- **Think of something slightly shocking but not too over the top:** You don't want to scare away or be too aggressive but you also don't want to fall flat. Be yourself but think a bit outside of the box. Be interesting and compelling and catch the guy off guard. This is a great way to get him to react because you have now grabbed his undivided attention and there is great possibility ahead. If you can find a way to do this successfully, then it makes for a really great platform to work off of moving forward.

- **Consider what might capture his interest based on what you know:** You may not know much about him, but try to appeal to what you know about him... even if it's just little stuff. If he seems interesting in a certain way or has a certain personality trait then appeal to that. It's all about knowing your audience, so perhaps you ask him to a movie that he might like. Maybe you mention something over your text about an area that you know is of particular interest to him. Maybe you invite him along to a game or try to make the first move based upon something that is totally what he is all about. It can be a great way to show interest, to grab his attention, and also to give you the foundation for a great first date or meeting.

- **Be sure that it's open-ended and ensures next steps or some type of interest:** Remember you want your text to make him want to text you back. You want something in that text to be compelling enough that he can't wait to reply back. This is a great way of expressing yourself in a noninvasive way that will be sure to show what you are all about. You need something you can leave behind in terms of next steps or some sort of action you want him to take. When you can get to that point then you are going to have great success and the back and forth conversation over text really begins—it's all about having a great opener!

# Chapter 6 - Should I Text Him First?

So the question comes up all the time as to when a girl should make the first move. This is an age old question, particularly as times are changing and women are more often taking the lead. If you find yourself in a situation where you are unsure of when to text him first specifically, there can be some good guidelines to help you make the right decision.

Whether you are outgoing or more introverted, it can be difficult to know when to make that important first move. If you find yourself unsure or maybe you're at a crossroads, then it's always good to go for it. The only reason to hold off is if you are playing a little hard to get or if you aren't getting that good positive vibe from it. In any other case, it's always fun to take the lead and send that first move.

Don't make it into more than it needs to be, for the very best way to show interest is to take the bull by the horns! If you feel a little apprehensive, try to turn that negative energy into positive instead. Here are a couple of things to help you get the courage and make that first and all important move.

- **When you want to really grab his attention and show your true interest:** If you are pretty sure about him and invested into trying things out, then go for it. If you want to really get his attention and make him stand up and take notice, then by all means send the first text. What do you have to lose here? It's always best to go for it and send a little interest than to wait for him. So if you are feeling it and you think that he is too, then get his attention and draw him in—a well planned out text is a great way to do just that!

- **When you want to be in the driver's seat and ensure that you make the first move:** Maybe you are sick of being in the passenger seat and you want to take control for a change. Maybe you feel like you are tired of waiting for him to make the first move and you want to take charge for a change. If you want to start off with a bit of control in a fun way, then send the first text. Again there is nothing to lose and everything to possibly gain, so put yourself out there and see how he reacts—just be ready for it!

- **When you think that it can show interest and really grab a positive reaction, therefore you have some confidence in the situation:** Sometimes you just feel it and you know that getting him to show interest will come if you send that first text. This can work if he happens to be shy or if you happen to be extraordinarily outgoing. This can work if you feel that he is going to reciprocate or if you genuinely just want to take the lead for a change.

This can also work if you want to get his attention and you are pretty confident that he'll react positively. If you have a basis for which to work off of, then go for it. There is always the potential for a letdown, but you will never know until you try— and in most instances you sending that first text is going to show interest and indicate that you are a really good one to talk to so he'll be interested and hooked!

# Chapter 7 - How to Really Keep His Attention

Okay so you've grabbed his attention and you have a nice back and forth dialogue going strong. You are really into him and he's really into you, and the foundation is starting to be laid. Things are going well, but you're only in the introductory phase—so how do you keep the momentum going? How can you continue to keep his attention after those first few exciting introductory texts?

Sometimes getting the attention and interest at the beginning is the easy part, but keeping it requires a bit more work. While texting can work really well for getting to know each other and to build up that attraction and chemistry, it does require a lot of work on both of your parts. If you let it flow naturally and keep things interesting and slightly evasive, then that's a good technique that will always pay off. If you can draw him in and keep him exactly where you want him to be, then that will show him that you are an intriguing girl that he will want to continue to get to know.

### *Keep the Positive and Fun Momentum Going Strong*

So if you find yourself being indecisive and where you really want to keep him interested, let this be a positive. Take the anxiety out of it and instead focus on being self assured and using texts to convey that. It might sound like a tall order, but if you are just yourself and you continue the fun momentum it will pay off tremendously. Here are a few things to keep in mind to keep it engaging, to keep his interest, and to see just where this can go.

- **Really enjoy the process of getting to know each other in this capacity:** Texting is a unique way of getting to know each other in a unique manner, so take advantage of it. Really enjoy what this process can be all about and embrace the way that you can talk to each other. Sure the texts are a brief and more straightforward way of communicating, but it can be so rewarding.

  The process is often the most exciting part, so keep him interested and balance it out. Not too many texts but also not too few either. Show him that yes you are interested, but that he has to work for it a little too! That balance will really pay off in the way that he interacts with you in the future!

- **Learn what to appeal to with him as an individual:** You are getting to know him and therefore learning about what makes him tick. Appeal to his senses, his interests, and the way that he is wired. Gear your texts towards things that are of interest to him, but also be sure to put forth your own unique individuality as well.

  When you can strike that fine accord and really enjoy placing texts that will continue to draw him in, it's very rewarding. If you know of a hobby or interest that he has then gear your texts towards it. Everybody is unique so find his core makeup and then the texts that you send will show that you are interested, which will inevitably be reciprocated.

- **Work off of each other's energy and keep it upbeat and intriguing:** It does take two, but when you are both in sync it really shows. Getting to know each other and having fun with this stage of the process is such a joy. Remain positive, take the time to really get to know each other, and continue to communicate through texts as well as verbally.

  Though this may be new to you in terms of dating and attraction, it gives you the opportunity to build a very important foundation. If the texts are successful then the dates and the relationship will continue to blossom off of this core foundation. So keep him interested and let him interest you as you are getting to know one another.

# Chapter 8 - Being Playful and Flirty

Texting can also be an excellent way to get into some real fun—the flirtaceous kind of fun! So many people assume that this is really what texting is all about when trying to find a guy. While it is a distinct advantage, and a fun one at that, there are other uses for this form of communication. When you get to this part of the equation however, it can be really great to run with it and enjoy the built up anticipation.

It is important to remember a few golden rules when it comes to texting in this capacity A lot of people think that flirting needs to be promiscuous and that's simply not true! Sure you can flirt and have fun and get to know each other, but that doesn't mean that you have to put too much out there. It also means that you don't have to be something that you're not!

This is like anything else within the texting arena, be yourself and get a bit outside of your comfort zone, but don't push it too much! Have fun and be flirty, but don't try too hard. Sort of let it flow naturally and then you will find that this makes for a much more comfortable experience, and that it tends to flow much better from his end as well. Keep the following in mind and you are going to love every minute of this fun and flirty stage.

- **Remember not to put all of your cards on the table:** Do have fun, do be flirtaceous, but also leave a bit to the imagination. If you put it all out there, particularly in text form, then he's probably going to lose interest. Men want a bit of a chase, and that holds particularly true with texting.

  Keep it interesting, make it fun and interesting for him, but do not put it all out there so that there is nothing left for him to wonder about. Remember that to keep him interested means that you give him a little bit of yourself at a time—remember that always and you'll be just fine.

- **When you are having fun with texting then it shows and works well towards playfulness:** It's the same sort of philosophy that when you're smiling, people can tell. Well the same idea holds true here in that when you are having fun and really enjoying yourself in a carefree and flirty type of way, he can pick up on that. Don't get too serious, don't throw yourself in whole heartedly, but just remember that this beginning stage is all about getting to know each other and doing some simple flirting.

Texting can be quite effective for that, so embrace it!

- **There's a fine line between being flirtaceous and being desperate or trampy—know it so you don't cross it:** Sure being flirty can be loads of fun, but you can also get carried away with it if you're not careful.

  Remember that there is a fine line between flirtaceous and trampy, and be able to recognize it when that occurs and never cross it. If you can keep sight of that then you are going to have fun with it. If you come across as too aggressive or trying too hard, then it can be misconstrued as desperate. Keep sight of what you want your texts to convey and keep it at that in the right style and tone.

- **Keep it light, carefree, playful, and fun and it sets the right tone:** If you can just look at this as another form of communication or way of getting yourself out there, then you can relax a bit. Be a vixen but in a fun way. Use this as a means by which you can chat it up and be flirty, but never take yourself too seriously. When you can find that fine line then you will know that you have done it right, and it will show in his captivated response and continued interest. This will also mean that you have taken things to the next level, and now the real fun with your guy begins!

# Chapter 9 - When to Be Seductive and When to Be Mysterious

There comes a time when you're ready to take your texts and your relationship to the next level. There's a time when you just KNOW that you are ready to take it to the next level, but you want to be sure that you do it in the right way. Though you may feel a bit uncertain or apprehensive, the truth is that this can be a really fun way to accelerate things!

As mentioned earlier, there is a fine line between being seductive and keeping things interesting and not pushing too hard too fast. You do want to insert a bit of seduction and intrigue into the mix because that's how texting helps you to move forward and have fun—this is where it can be a helpful tool. If used properly then it can work wonders for moving your relationship forward!

***Finding the Balance between Interest and Pushing Too Hard Is Important***

Being seductive can and should still be a bit mysterious. This is where you want to be sure that you don't come across as desperate or try too hard, but rather grab his attention. No matter what the tone of the relationship has been up until now, you can really speed things up in a super fun way—but be sure that it's all about seduction and trying to be intimate but never too much too fast!

If you feel unsure about how to accomplish this as so many girls do, here are some guidelines to help you know when not to proceed to this next level. These can point you towards what it means to be fun, playful, seductive, and suggestive but NEVER put it all out there or take the risk of coming on too strong—always be a bit mysterious and be aware of the situation before you try this out.

- **If you feel that he is not reciprocating, then you may want to back off a little bit:** Let him work for it a little bit because otherwise it's going to get old fast for both of you. It needs to be a two-sided thing and you need to get that "vibe" from him, and if you're not then back of a little bit. Seduction can be a great tactic for moving things forward, but you need to be sure that he's into you and that he's feeling it too. Otherwise hold off for a bit and let him wonder a little!

- **If you feel like things are moving too fast and you're not ready for it, then slow it down:** It might be you that isn't ready to take it to that next step, and so you need to put the brakes on if you feel that way. If things feel like they are moving too fast then do not go to the seductive phase because it will set unrealistic expectations. Be truthful and just back off a bit, but still show interest if you want to see where things go. This is like anything else and when you are in the driver's seat, it's a good thing where relationships are concerned.

- **When you can find that balance between being coy and showing him that you want him, then that's the perfect spot:** This is the best possible place for this phase! When you can show him that you are interested and show a bit of seduction and flirting, but yet you can pull back enough to make him want you more!

This is where the attraction really starts to blossom and where you can start to really make this all your own. You will know when you've struck that fine balance when you see that he keeps pursuing you and the chemistry is alive and well. This is often where the relationship starts to progress and next steps naturally occur.

# Chapter 10 - Things NOT To Say

Okay, so with all of the good you know there has to be some bad too. Sad but true, all of us have to be told what NOT to say sometimes. It's not to say that you would put yourself out there in theory, but sometimes when we get comfortable and we get wrapped up in everything we have a tendency to say things that are not our norm. Love makes you do crazy things, no matter what level you might be at!

When you see some of the items on the list they may seem obvious. Who would say these things? Isn't it obvious that you don't want to put it all out there in a text? While that's true in theory, the reality is that these texting mistakes are more common than you might realize. So in order to prevent dating disasters, avoid these at all costs.

### These Texts Could Cause Epic Failure, So Don't Fall Into the Trap!

If you want to keep the attraction going then don't make these mistakes. Even if they seem innocent enough or if you are sure that you're at this point in the relationship, try not to be in this position ever.

1. **I miss you, when can we spend more time together?** This is like an open invitation to rejection, so don't do it. Sure it seems sweet and innocent enough, but if you put this out there then there's no wonder left. You need to keep a bit of mystery and make him want to work for it more.

   If you tell him you miss him and ask him to spend more time with you, then you come across needy. Don't be that girl, be the one that he is seeking out and that he wants to spend more time with. Being a bit of a challenge is always a good thing and always manages to keep things interesting and fresh.

2. **What are you doing, why can't I reach you?** Anything accusatory that makes him feel like he's on the defensive will never be received well. Even if you feel mad and you are warranted in that, don't show it through text. Also be very aware of the stage that you are at in your relationship.

   If you are asking too many questions about his whereabouts or trying to make him answer you when he's not at that stage, then he's not going to budge. Never start a text with something that will make him feel smothered or put him in a defensive position. It's not good for him and it's going to make you look desperate, which is never a good thing.

3. **What stage do you think our relationship is at?** First and foremost this is not the type of question that you want to text to him, so keep that in mind. Secondly when you are putting this out there, particularly early in a relationship, it's never going to go well. He's probably not ready for this question and now it's coming across as needy, desperate and clingy—not good at all! Save this conversation for the right time and place, and never use texting for it. Do be careful in general for asking this question at the wrong time can send him packing.

4. **I love you!** If you are already deep into the relationship and feel confident about this, then great. If you already say this to each other and it's a natural extension, then wonderful. If however this is the first time that you're saying it or if you are unsure of his reaction, do NOT send it by text. This will be something that you want to say face to face when the time is right. Texting it, particularly if you are uncertain of his reaction, is never ever going to be a good idea.

5. **It's the middle of the night, do you want to come over?** This is what everyone will refer to as a booty

call, so don't be that girl! If you start down this path then this is the way that it will go. You may very well move onto a physical relationship, but be sure that the time is right. Texting something like this in the middle of the night will not earn you respect, and could actually cost you the good parts of the relationship. Never be somebody that he can use, and don't put this out there on text. Again make him work for it and sending a text such as this will never work out that way. Think before you text always!

# Chapter 11 - Handling Misinterpretations and Other Common Texting Problems

The only downside to texting when it comes to dating and attraction is the fact that it is often the source of a lot of misinterpretations. Though you may not mean something a certain way, you are working with a limited amount of text, and it can come across with a totally different intent. That just goes to show that you need to be mindful of the texts that you send and prepared for any misreading.

There are some common texting problems that you should be aware of and ready for. Though you want to strive not to make these common mistakes, sometimes just being proactive can help you out of a bad situation. No matter what, thinking through a recovery strategy if you think there's a problem can always be a good thing.

*Being Proactive Can Save a Big Headache Later*

Here are a few things that can help out of the biggest and most common texting dilemmas. It's not just you that goes through this, and so if you recognize this you can salvage things and get back on track.

- **Always think about how your texts could be interpreted:** If you take the time to think through what your text might mean to a guy, then you will avoid this type of situation altogether. If you can be proactive in this manner, then a crisis is usually averted. Since we're girls, we almost never think about things from a guy's point of view though, but it's a good practice. When you are new to dating this guy always try to think like he might and consider how your text might interpreted by him. This is a good technique no matter what stage you are at in the relationship, but especially at first.

- **Be prepared to discuss what you really meant if it's not taken that way:** If the text comes off in a certain undesired way then be prepared to talk it out. Sometimes good communication like this can really put the two of you in a good place. This can also serve as an excellent foundation in the first place, so talking it out even when there's not an issue is a good approach. If however something comes up that could cause a potential problem, talk it out and tell him what you really meant. Honesty speaks volumes!

- **Be sure that you are also using different ways of communicating:** Though texting can be such an excellent form of communicating, be sure that it's not your ONLY form of communication! Be sure that you are talking on the phone, through email, and/or face-to-face. If you rely only on text alone that can be a relationship killer almost instantly. Use texting to convey fun thoughts and get the attraction going, but then be sure that you are getting to know each other in different ways as well. This will really pay off!

- **Save some chats for face to face and talk through any hard feelings:** If there are hot issues to discuss or if you think that something is better left said in person, then go with your gut. Chances are that if you are concerned about the chat over text, then it's not the right venue. While texting can be a great way of putting yourself out there and developing a bond, some things are better to say in person to ensure that there are no misconceptions or miscommunications.

- **Know that sometimes texting can present common issues and don't let that put a wrench in things:** If you are at least aware of it then you can prepare for it. Know that the most common texting issues come in the way of misinterpretations and possible hard feelings. Know this, work through it, and be mindful of it when you send your texts. Have a strategy in place to talk through anything that came off right. If you are unsure of how a text may convey something, then save it for a different form of communicating. Keep these things in mind and you are always going to end up in a good situation, and that's what really matters! Use texting the way that it was intended, and it will always work FOR you and never against you.

# Chapter 12 - Is "Sexting" A Good Idea?

It's an inevitable direction that comes up with every good texting relationship. It's something that a lot of people perceive that texting is used for in the first place. It's gotten a lot of attention, mostly negative, and yet it can be a way to keep the relationship alive and well. Its sexting and it has taken over the world of texting and changed the way that people interact, both good and bad. But is it a good idea for you? Is this something that you should focus on within your own relationship? There are some important things to keep in mind when it comes to this subject.

Let's start by recognizing that sexting as it has become known is not for everyone. Though texting alone can help you to come out of your shell, this particular form of texting can really take things to a whole new level. If you are somebody that can feel comfortable in this realm, then that's great and you should enjoy it. If however it pushes you so far out of your comfort zone that you feel anxious or even stressed, then it may be wise to avoid it.

*It's Not for Everyone and That's Okay To Admit*

There is no doubt that sexting will take the relationship to a whole new level, and it may be one that you are unprepared for. Not only is this a form of intimacy, but it can leave you feeling very exposed. When done between two people that are into this and interested, it can be a great way to highlight that connection and chemistry. Done with even one of the parties feeling uncomfortable, it can make for a very bad choice within the relationship as a whole. Either way you want to really evaluate this before you ever do it!

Do recognize that this can be a great way to jumpstart the relationship and get things heading in a positive and physical direction. If you really want to enjoy an exciting platform, then this is the way to get there. You do need to know though that these texts are now public record, meaning that trust needs to be inherent so that the texts are not shared with anybody else. This is just another thing to consider with sexting so that you make the right choice.

So if you are somebody who enjoys putting herself out there like this and are prepared for where this heads things, then this can be an excellent way of enjoying things. If however you are not sure of what this will do to you or your relationship, then stay away from it at all costs! Just be sure that you know what this will do and then if you decide to do it, enjoy it for all that it can be.

### *Be Ready For Where This Can Lead or Don't Do It At All*

Here are some important things to consider as you evaluate if sexting is right for you or for your blooming relationship—just evaluate and make the right choice!

- **If you have doubt, then DON'T do it:** This is a good rule of thumb because if you feel at all unsure then it's best to stay away from this altogether. Though you may not think that some sexually explicit texts can be harmful, they can. If you are unsure or feel pressured or that it could cause a negative outcome, then don't do it! This is one thing that you need to be very sure of or it will end in disaster!

- **If you can keep it light, fun, and carefree without negative feelings then go for it:** This is not a time to try for more in the relationship, but rather to keep it carefree. Sexting is all about building up the anticipation and therefore having fun with it. This is about extending your chemistry and heading in a very positive physical direction. If you are going to get too emotionally invested or "heavy" with this form of texting, then it's best not to even start. Again, keeping it light-hearted is the key here!

- **If you are at a good point in the relationship to bring out this form of intimacy and communication, then try it out:** You are your own best judge and so if this feels like the next natural step then it may be worth a try. If you feel that the relationship isn't there yet or if you are unready for intimacy at all yet, then it's definitely not the right time! You will know when it's the right time and until you get there, you need to completely avoid this subject.

- **If you are unsure of things, feel they are moving too fast, or worried about any red flags then hold off:** Any red flags or signs that things are not heading in a positive direction are to be paid attention to. Be sure to take a step back and be honest with yourself, and if things are moving too fast or you're not ready to take it "there" yet, then don't. If you are dealing with a good guy then he will understand and respect that. If however it's not a good match then this will show itself if you level with him. Sexting can be a lot of fun and a great natural catalyst for a physical relationship, but only if you are truly ready and you are both a good match for each other—so do an honest evaluation to make sure this is the right thing for you!

# Chapter 13 - Developing and Nurturing a Good Two-Way Texting Relationship

If you haven't picked up on it yet, the way that you interact and develop a good dialogue can be so important. That means that it needs to be two of you going back and forth, and developing a good relationship by talking things through as a couple. It doesn't matter what stage of the relationship that you are at. When you are getting to know each other, this takes time and a lot of nurturing. Texts can be the perfect complimentary form of communication at every stage of a long-lasting relationship!

The important thing to remember though is that this should never be a one-sided. If you feel that he is doing all the texting and that you aren't really feeling that chemistry, then perhaps it's time to evaluate your interest level. If alternatively you are the one doing all of the texting and you don't feel as though you are getting much in the way of a reaction or dialogue, then perhaps he's feeling that same concern. This should be an open dialogue and exchange of texts between two people that are truly interested!

*This Should Work As a Positive and Helpful Part of the Relationship*

When you take a step back and really consider it, texting is another way of communicating and makes for a great avenue for keeping things interesting. It's a true exchange between you and your guy and keeping each other interested and exploring your relationship. This should be a positive way of getting closer and getting to appreciate each other even more! And if you allow it to be such then you will enjoy where it can take you.

So if your texting is truly two-way then it means success. If you're not feeling it or fear that he's not feeling it, then the texting may not be doing the best job of communication. This may mean that more face-to-face communication is necessary, or it may mean that you are not a good match. If you are unsure of how to evaluate this or how to get to this phase, then here are some helpful guidelines to keep in mind and use as you are moving forward.

- **Learn to look for cues from him for best reactions:** As you get to know him and he gets to know you, it will become apparent when there are certain cues. You will get to know what to expect from each other in the way of communication and in the way of personalities as a whole. If you can look for cues then you will know when to send texts and when to wait for him. This is how the chemistry evolves and how the relationship blossoms between you, and texting can be a great catalyst for all of that—just be sure to always be on the lookout for cues and getting to know each other well.

- **Be sure that this is a true dialogue and never one-sided:** If you are feeling that things are one-sided, then back off a bit. This doesn't mean that you're not interested or that you're playing "hard to get" but rather that you are keeping things interesting.

   Sometimes giving that brief space can make him stand up and take notice, and then you'll get that text that you've been waiting for. Do be sure that you are evaluating things properly and being really honest with yourself. If you are feeling that a little delay in texting him is necessary, then follow your gut. Sometimes this can make for a nice way for him to miss you and for the texts to get even more interesting. Just being perceptive can always pay off!

- **Take the time to get to know each other and keep this form of conversation fun and a good source of a connection:** Texts when placed properly can be a fundamental way of communicating and getting to know each other better. So be sure that you keep that in mind and use it in the appropriate manner. When you can do that then you will know and feel when it's successfully working. This is like email or phone calls and is another way of talking and getting to know each other.

It's a great way to keep things interesting and light, and a really fun way to build up the attraction. You want to use this to nurture and strengthen things and really enjoy what this can do for you. Texting can take your relationship to the next level, but be sure that you are both engaged and using it to the best of its ability. When you can do that, then you can really get to enjoy this form of communication and getting to know each other and building great chemistry—it really does work when you allow it to!

# Chapter 14 - The Power of Suggestion

If you aren't aware of it per se or if you are not sure of how it really works, then understanding the true power of suggestion can be key point to understand. This is the idea that sometimes saying less is really more in the way of a relationship. This is where being coy or evasive can actually show him that you are interested AND interesting. This is how you can really keep the good chemistry between you two and continue to keep that going as you get to know each other better. This is where what you say and how you say it can matter so much!

When you put texts out there and really utilize this form of communication for all that it can be, then you can get to the heart of what texting is all about. This isn't like the alternative where you can write a small novel through email or talk each other's ear off over the phone. You have a limited amount of space to say what you are thinking and what you want to convey, and so you really want to make it count and work the right way. When you can do this, then you will know that you are in control of this way of communicating and that's a beautiful thing.

***Simple is Often Better Especially in This Capacity***

So keep in mind that the idea is that the text is a short way of conveying what you want to say. It's a great way of staying connected and yet it's really all about keeping things interesting. It's a simple but very effective way of igniting the chemistry and keeping it strong throughout. So here are some helpful ways to ensure that happens and that you keep the text short, to the point, and full of the power of suggestion at work:

- **Recognize that a little goes a long way:** The idea of "less is more" is truly alive and well here. If you want to keep him interested then a little truly does go a long way. Don't get carried away or try to say too much in your texts. Never use your texts as a substitute for other ways of chatting. Do be sure that the right words give off the right message and attitude. So keep it simple, keep it light, keep it brief, and pack the meaning into fewer words. Less is more and this is really the best example of that, and can work as a philosophy to keep in mind when moving forward with your guy.

- **You want to keep him coming back for more, and your texts should be an extension of that:** The power of suggestion means that you are saying something without ever saying it at all. So that in turn means that your texts should be well planned out to keep him wanting more. This is something that you'll want to convey in person by being coy and playful, and then your texts should be a direct extension of that. If you can keep him on the edge of his seat and enjoying this playful vibe, then your texts can be considered truly successful and well played!

- **Never give away too much, always keep him intrigued or it won't end well:** If you put it all out there, then what's going to keep him interested? Keep it fun and informative, but never give away too much information on your texts. If you can keep that in mind then you will never allow yourself to get too carried away with what you say in your texts. Find that right balance and strike it, so that he's intrigued, wants to keep things going, you want to keep getting to know each other, and the chemistry is alive and well and building. It's a fine balance but you CAN strike it!

- **This helps to create a good foundation for getting to know each other well without laying everything out there from the start:** Whether you realize it or not the power of suggestion can go a long way in building up a great foundation. You are getting to know each other, yet the well placed and coy texts can keep it very interesting. So there's a natural connection and chemistry that you are feeling with each other and that transforms and manifests itself into a great relationship.

This is important at the beginning as the foundation is being built, but continues to be important as you are trying to keep things strong and intact for the future. The relationship will naturally evolve and you don't have to work too hard at it, and the right texts will help you through every step of the way. It's an amazing feeling when it is all going well and finally working together just right!

# Chapter 15 - Balancing Virtual vs. Face-to-Face Communications

There's a time and a place for everything, or so they say. That same sort of philosophy holds true when it comes to the need for texting over other forms of communication. Knowing when the time is right or when a face-to-face conversation makes more sense is all part of the learning process. You will gain this insight and experience as you move forward. You will learn when you need to have that personal contact or when a well placed text can do the trick. Either way, it's up to you to get a read on where things are at and what might work best.

This isn't always cut and dry, and it's dependent in large part on the personalities of the two people in the relationship. Sometimes communicating simple messages over text works just fine the majority of the time. Other times these texts can be easily misconstrued or read wrong, and that means that a personal conversation makes far more sense. It's up to you to focus on what works for the two of you and then proceed accordingly.

***Be In Tune to What Works For Different Situations***

There are cues or ways of detecting what is going to keep you going in the right direction. If you can really get a sense for what makes the communication run smoothly, then you can really find this fine balance. It may seem difficult at first, but as you get to know each other better and get a real sense of what makes the other person tick, it will come more naturally. It's a balancing act for sure, and you are both going to make some mistakes along the way—and that's okay and part of the relationship process!

This all serves well in creating a solid foundation for your relationship and for how things move forward. So if you feel unsure of what the fine line is between a virtual vs. a face-to-face conversation, then here are some things to help you to determine which course makes the most sense.

- **Texts should be an extension to face-to-face communication:** Neither should be a substitute but rather a nice extension. If you can learn to focus on talking in various mediums in this way, then you can get them both to work for you. This means that you know when the simple but well placed text will work, and when you get a sense of when a good conversation can work better.

  You aren't necessarily going to know this right off the bat, but rather it takes time to learn it. So recognize first and foremost that texts should be a good extension of your conversations in person.

They should be a further and perhaps more carefree way of getting to know each other and building attraction—they are never a substitute for talking, but rather another nice way to do it!

- **Texts should be used to convey simple thoughts and keep the momentum going:** These are the simple thoughts that say so much, but in very little words. Remember that when it comes to texting less is more, whereas in face to face conversation you want to get more in depth. This represents a major difference and can therefore help you to get to the points that you want to cover within each form of communication. Never put too much into your texts or they will become boring, monotonous, or just ignored because you are using them incorrectly.

- **Face-to-face communication helps to further build the chemistry and keep things strong:** You need that personal contact to help keep the chemistry going strong and build the momentum. You need to see things like eye contact, facial expressions, smiles, suggestive hints and body language that texts can't capture. Therefore the face time is so important to help cement things and ensure that the chemistry and the foundation are strong and intact. Texting is great in the initial dating and flirting stages of a relationship but it can only grow when you have personal interactions with your guy.

- **Texting and face-to-face communication used together can build great chemistry and keep the relationship moving along quite well:** The combination of well placed texts with a good interpersonal dynamic makes for strong attraction, an excellent foundation, and a really good start for almost any relationship. Get them to all work together and there is no stopping you! These two will work together to convey your thoughts, help you to get to know each other, and really work to make you a stronger couple.

No matter where you are at in the relationship, the combination of really strong and effective texts with a solid and working face-to-face communication can help the attraction to grow and make the relationship work on so many different fronts. Try it and see for yourself how well it all just works together!

# Chapter 16 - Great Sample Texts

Suffice it to say that every relationship and every couple is different. The reality is that these sample texts can be good idea starters, but the rest is up to you. Use these to help get you started in the right direction, but then recognize that it's up to you to decide what will work given your personalities and the current stage of the relationship. Messages that may work for some may not work for everyone.

These examples offer a good solid starting point thought if you feel clueless, and they all represent various examples of what good texts can and should do. Though you may not feel comfortable in one particular area, the others may be just what you want. So take a look and really focus on what the core message is, and then cater it to your own specific situation.

### *Good Idea Starters - The Rest is Up To You*

Having an idea of what makes up some great texts can ensure that you go down the right path and keep the attraction and relationship going strong. When you can put forth your thoughts in this manner, it really shows good effort and builds up the attraction and interest. He will be intrigued when you put forth that perfectly timed and worded text, and then the rest is history.

So here are a few good sample texts that can get you started depending on where you are at in the dating and relationship process.

### "Hey, where are you watching the game later?"

Asking a question, being slightly suggestive, and yet raising his interest—and so it works well. You are not putting him on the defensive, but what you are doing is showing interest in something that clearly interests him. You are suggesting that you might like to watch the game with him without ever saying those words.

This is a good way to communicate interest in a subtle way that is sure to grab his attention, show him that you are interested in him and what he likes, and yet not coming across as needy or desperate. You are laid back and willing to maybe join him, but not coming right out to say it—and this all works!

### "This weekend was a lot of fun"

You had a great time and its okay to let him know that. You're not getting into specifics and you're not coming across as needy. You're stating a fact and hopefully getting him to reflect on and remember the fun that he had too. It's a great way to get yourself fresh in his mind throughout the day, and to make him want to have that same fun with you again whatever it was.

### *"You crack me up, still thinking about last night"*

Evasive and yet effective, this message works like a charm. Remind him of something that he said or did, that likely only the two of you know about, made you laugh and it's good to put it out there. You are stroking his ego as you compliment his humor and you are keeping yourself fresh in his mind. This is great as the relationship is just starting to form and makes him smile and think about you when he's away from you.

### *"I wish I was still in bed"*

Do you mean with him? Do you just mean that you're tired or something more? This is a perfect example of a coy text that gets him to thinking. It's sure to be met with just as coy of a response if you two are on the same page. This can be a great way to test the waters and to see what kind of reaction that you get. It's a fun way of keeping the interest and momentum going, and to see what you might be met with.

### *"Your place or mine?"*

This is great if you are already in a good place relationship wise. It can lead to further conversation or actions, but just be sure that you are to this point already. It's obvious that you are hinting at something more physical in nature. If you are feeling confident or have taken your relationship to a new level, then this is a great way of flirting without being obvious or saying too much. Just be sure you are ready for this!

### *"You are really good….at making a girl happy"*

He's going to smile when he reads this. You are having fun, you are carefree and light, and yet you are also stroking his ego at the same time. This is the perfect type of text to send after there is already a sort of familiarity between the two of you. It can work wonders for getting him to want more and to stay interested. Saying a lot with very little words—proof that less really is more!

### *"I can't stop smiling…wonder why that is?!"*

You are clearly comfortable with each other at this point, and you share some special experience or inside jokes together. You are fun and he is having fun with you. At this point you are feeling good about things and you can really let yourself feel freer. He is sure to respond with something equally as charming, and the momentum just keeps growing and building. It's a great thing when you get to this point with your texts!

### *"Can't wait for tonight"*

This is to the point and that works when are comfortable with each other. This could be about some big plans you have for that night or something a bit more in depth. The only ones that actually know the true meaning of this text are the two of you. This means that the attraction and relationship are in a very good place. This type of text serves well for helping him to think about you during the day in the right way, and that's always a good thing.

# Conclusion

Texting a great way of communicating, and is here to stay. Texting serves so many wonderful purposes in communication, and it can offer a very positive element when it comes to attracting and dating a guy. There are some do's and don'ts as we have pointed out here, but if used properly texting can really help to build interest and keep the momentum going within a good relationship.

You do want to use texting as a way of extending the communication, but of course never as a substitution for face-to-face interactions. Texts are great for sending simple, brief, and concise thoughts that keep things interesting and fun. They should be carefree and light, and always work to strengthen his interest. When your texts find that perfect balance you will know it and the rest will come together quite nicely.

The right texts can work to strengthen things and to make him want to get to know you better. Be sure of the stage of your relationship that you are at before you send certain types of texts. Always work within the confines of what you feel comfortable with, and though you do want to push it a little bit, you don't ever want to create anxiety with your texts. Keep in mind what works for you and what will make for a good match for the two of you, and then you can't go wrong.

Texting can be an excellent way of generating attraction and strengthen the dating and relationship journey. Just be sure that you use it properly, be yourself, and have fun with it. Never make your texts too heavy and this will always keep him interested and ensure that you can take things exactly where you want to go!

*Enjoy texting for all that it can be, and watch how it can strengthen your attraction and make for a good foundation within your relationship—best of luck!*